Panel from Longton Swimming Bath, painted by Albert Slater, 1886, now on permanent display at the City Museum and Art Gallery, Hanley, Stoke on Trent.

VICTORIAN TILES

Hans van Lemmen

Shire Publications Ltd

CONTENTS

Set in 10 on 9 point Times and printed in Great Britain by C. I. Thomas & Sons (Haverfordwest) Ltd, Press Buildings, Merlins Bridge, Haverfordwest.

ACKNOWLEDGEMENTS

The author wishes to thank Mr G. K. Beaulah for his many valuable comments throughout the writing of this book and for the loan of tiles illustrated in this book, Mr J. Rumsby for the use of tiles from his private collection, and the Gladstone Pottery Museum, Stoke-on-Trent, and Hull Museums for permission to photograph tiles in their collections. Illustrations are acknowledged as follows: Mr G. K. Beaulah, pages 4 (top two, middle left), 5 (left), 7, 9; Mr J. Rumsby, pages 15 (bottom right), 18 (top right), 22 (top left), 23 (top left, middle right); Hull Museums, pages 20, 21. The remaining illustrations are from the author's collection.

BELOW: *Block-printed tile, black transfer, no marks, c 1890. The strong simplification of form has an Arts and Crafts inspired influence about it.*

Hand-made and hand-painted tile with blue leaves and orange fruit, made by J. van Hulst, Harlingen, Holland, catalogue pattern number 734, c 1885. The handling of the design reveals the influence of the Arts and Crafts Movement.

INTRODUCTION

Victorian tiles are being rediscovered by many people for different reasons. The attractive decorative qualities of Victorian tiles have caught the attention of collectors, but students of Victorian architecture and design are equally interested in Victorian tiles because tiles performed such an important function in nineteenth-century architecture and the wealth of different patterns on tiles throws much light on the change in and development of decorative styles and taste in the Victorian era. Museums up and down Britain have begun forming their own collections of nineteenth-century tiles and there have been exhibitions throughout Britain. People suddenly discover that the tiles they have in their fireplace or porch are Victorian tiles that are worth looking at and reading about. Because of large-scale demolition in Victorian towns many tiles have found their way into antique shops but unfortunately much has been lost and many serious collectors and students of Victorian tiles now realise that the documentation of tiles *in situ* in the form of accurate descriptions and photographs is as important as the collecting of tiles themselves. It is hoped that this book will make many more people aware of the visually interesting qualities of Victorian tiles and that it will lead to more extensive collecting and preservation *in situ*.

3

Medieval and Dutch and English Delftware tiles: (top to bottom and left to right) Meaux Abbey, c 1250; Walton Abbey, c 1280; seventeenth-century Dutch polychrome tile; eighteenth-century Dutch blue-and-white tile; eighteenth-century blue-and-white Liverpool tiles.

4

Printed tiles decorated by John Sadler of Liverpool: (left) tile with a print taken from a woodblock, 1756; (right) tile with a print taken from a copper-plate, c 1760.

PRE VICTORIAN TILES

Tilemaking in Britain goes back to the middle ages when many abbey churches and later parish churches began to use inlaid tiles as floor coverings, adding new colour to church interiors. The production of medieval inlaid tiles began in the thirteenth century and lasted until the Dissolution of the monasteries at the beginning of the sixteenth century. The medieval inlaid tile was made of red-firing clay and was decorated by means of an impression cut or stamped into the clay; after that white pipe clay was poured into the hollows. Following a period of air drying the tile was then scraped level, covered with a transparent lead glaze and fired. After firing the reddish clay and white pipe clay looked brown-red and yellow-white respectively.

After the Dissolution of the monasteries the craft of making inlaid tiles died out and it was not until the end of the seventeenth century that the next development occurred. During the seventeenth century the technique of making tin-glazed earthenware had come to England from Holland and with it had also come the technique of making tin-glazed wall tiles. The Dutch produced in very great numbers the characteristic blue-and-white Delftware tiles which they used on a large scale in their houses in cellars, as wall skirtings and in fireplaces. They also exported a lot of these tiles to many European countries, including England. English potters began to produce tiles very similar to the Dutch ones. Lambeth near London, Bristol and Liverpool became the three main production centres of English Delftware tiles during the eighteenth century. Although the main colour combination was blue motifs painted on white, they could also be executed in purple (manganese) on white, a combination of blue and purple on white, or in such colours as yellow, green, blue and orange. Unlike medieval tiles, which were fired only once, Delftware tiles needed two firings before they were finished. The tile squares were cut out of rolled and flattened clay, left to dry and then fired. They came out of the kiln as *biscuit* tiles. These biscuit tiles were then given a white tin glaze, after which the blue or other coloured decoration was painted on. The tile was then fired again, turning the glaze into an opaque glass-like substance, impervious to water from the front. Popular decorations were landscapes, biblical scenes, flowers, birds and people in a landscape setting.

An interesting development in the decoration technique of English Delftware tiles took place in the middle of the eighteenth century in Liverpool. In 1756 John Sadler with the aid of Guy Green perfected a way of transferring engraved prints to the surface of glazed white tiles. A thin piece of paper was used to transfer the printed image from an engraved metal plate to the tile. This method, known as *transfer printing*, became an important technique of tile decoration in the nineteenth century as it was cheap and could be done much more quickly than any form of hand painting. Towards the end of the eighteenth century the fashion for both hand-painted and printed Delftware tiles declined and although the tradition of tilemaking reappeared again during the late 1830s, it was then in the form of the thick and heavy inlaid floor tile rather than the thin and delicate painted and printed tinglazed tile.

EARLY VICTORIAN TILEMAKERS

Between the end of the eighteenth century and 1840 virtually no tiles were produced in Britain. L. Jewitt in his *The Ceramic Art of Great Britain* mentions that Peter Stephans, who carried on a pottery at Jackfield near Ironbridge at the beginning of the nineteenth century, made encaustic tiles as well as other pottery, but it was not until Herbert Minton had completed his experiments with making inlaid tiles that any commercial production took place.

The Minton firm was established by Thomas Minton in 1793. It was his son Herbert who became interested in reviving the craft of making inlaid tiles. Inlaid tiles were produced in great quantities during the middle ages but all the specialised local knowledge had been lost and could only be regained by trial and error. Another potter, Samuel Wright, had been working on the same problem independently of Herbert Minton, and Wright had taken out a patent for the production of *encaustic tiles* (this was the technical term for this class of tile throughout the nineteenth century) but his experiments met with little success. Herbert Minton bought a share in the patent and began to develop and perfect the technique.

The process of making an inlaid tile is as follows. Plastic clay was pushed into a square mould with a raised pattern at the bottom. When the tile came out of the mould, the pattern was indented in the tile. The tile was left to dry and then liquid clay (slip) of a different colour was poured into the hollows of the indented design. The tile was left to dry again and the surface then smoothed level with a knife. The problem was to find clays that have a similar contraction rate during firing and that was one of the main stumbling blocks Minton tried to overcome. He spent most of the 1830s trying to perfect the technique. It is ironic that Minton spent so much time and money trying to regain the lost skills of making inlaid tiles when just across the Channel in West Flanders there existed a flourishing local inlaid tile industry. Between St Omer (France) and Poperinge (Belgium) many local potters made inlaid floor and wall tiles which were used frequently in farmhouses in floors and fireplaces. The inlaid tile with the Flemish lion is one of the most characteristic.

Minton's persistence met with success and during the 1840s he was able to begin the commercial production of inlaid tiles. In 1842 he published a catalogue entitled *Old English Tile Designs,* which featured tiles based on medieval examples, particularly on the medieval tiles found in Westminster Abbey chapter house. Minton was greatly encouraged in his endeavours by Welby Pugin, the famous Gothic Revival architect, who advocated the use of inlaid floor tiles for Gothic Revival churches. On several occasions he designed tiles for Minton. During the 1840s and 1850s Minton received some important commissions. In 1841 he supplied tiles for the floor of Temple Church in London, in 1844 his firm made a decorative pavement for Osborne House, Queen Victoria's residence in the Isle of Wight, and during

Inlaid Minton floor tiles made between 1850 and 1868. The tile with the lion has a date mark of 1868 but the design appeared in Minton's first pattern book of 1835.

7

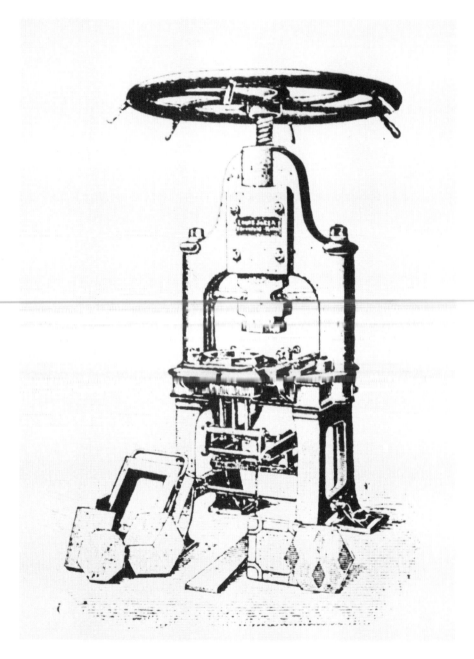

Tile press used for the manufacture of dust-pressed tiles (taken from L. Lefevre's 'Architectural Pottery', 1900).

Early printed Copeland tiles: (top to bottom and left to right) blue transfer print, c 1835; blue transfer print, the printed border suggesting that it has been used as part of a wall panel, c 1835; black transfer print with added hand colour simulating mosaic, c 1835; black transfer print with added hand colour simulating embroidery, c 1840.

the second half of the 1840s Minton tiles were used to pave the corridors at Westminster.

Herbert Minton also had an eye for the commercial potential of other inventions. One of the most important connected with tilemaking was the invention of clay dust pressing by Richard Prosser in 1840. He had developed a method of producing ceramic buttons by means of compressing slightly moist powdered clay between two metal dies in a press. The objects came out perfectly formed and needed only a very short drying period before they could be fired. Minton realised the potential of this method for the production of tiles and bought a share in the patent. The clay dust pressing process became of increasing importance from 1840 onwards and by the end of the nineteenth century most tiles were dust-pressed.

Other early Victorian tile manufacturers were Chamberlain's of Worcester and Copeland and Garrett. Chamberlain and Company produced inlaid tiles and were active between 1836 and 1840, when they were succeeded by G. Barr and Fleming St John. This manufacturer together with Herbert Minton bought Wright's patent when it came up for renewal in 1844. G. Barr and Fleming St John were taken over by H. Maw in 1850. Maw moved from Worcester to Broseley in 1852 and made his company one of the most important producers of the century. Copeland and Garrett, of Stoke-on-Trent, were active between 1833 and 1847 making encaustic tiles and also produced some early transfer-printed tiles. Between 1847 and 1867 they were known as W. T. Copeland and from 1867 onwards as W. T. Copeland and Sons. The early transfer-printed Copeland tiles are interesting since they show that rather than creating special designs for tiles existing plate patterns were used, although soon after they began to produce designs and patterns specially for tiles. The Copeland pattern books still exist and provide revealing insights into the general development of tile design. If dust-pressing tiles became one of the main techniques in the making of tiles, transfer printing became one of the main methods of decorating them.

THE TILE BOOM OF 1870 TO 1910

By 1870 inlaid tiles were used very extensively in churches, public buildings and large private houses. The production possibilities had been increased by an invention patented by Boulton and Worthington in 1863 which enabled inlaid tiles to be made by the dust-pressing method, although the more conventional plastic clay method continued to be used as well. In 1868 Minton had broken up into two distinct firms. The original tile business was run by Minton Hollins and Company, marking their inlaid tiles with the name *Minton & Co* and their wall tiles with the name *Minton Hollins & Co.* The other part of the Minton firm continued with the production of earthenware and porcelain, and although they did not make inlaid tiles they began the production of decorative wall tiles during the 1870s and some of their printed series have now an accredited place in the history of Victorian tiles. They marked their tiles with the name *Mintons China Works.* Both Minton Hollins and Company and Mintons China Works found themselves now competing against other firms such as Maw and Company, W. Godwin, the Architectural Pottery Company, T. and R. Boote, Malkin Edge and Company and even Wedgwood, which took up the production of tiles during the 1870s, but there seemed to be a big enough market, which expanded even more during the 1880s.

The housing boom of the 1880s and 1890s led to a remarkable increase in the demand for tiles and the existing firms were joined by a host of others mainly producing plain and decorative wall tiles. Victorian tiles must be considered in their architectural context because mostly they are a functional accessory with an important role within the total make-up of a Victorian building. The decorative aspect is subsidiary in this context although it has now become a prime factor for the collector. With the tightening up of building standards by local authorities the glazed tile came into its own as a surface which was easily cleaned and therefore very hygienic. Town halls, hospitals, libraries, railway stations, museums and so on show extensive use of floor and wall tiles and the use of tiles in houses both large and small now also became very common. Victorian houses of this period had tiles in the hall, tiles in the bathroom and behind the sink in the kitchen and as part of hearths and fireplace surrounds. Tiles were also used in furniture like wash stands, chairs, sideboards and umbrella stands. Shops such as butchers and fishmongers were often tiled throughout in white for hygiene but frequently large decorative panels with

The porch of a house in Hull with glazed wall tiles and plain and inlaid floor tiles, c 1885.

scenes depicting farm animals or the fishing industry were incorporated and several such shop interiors are still extant. Plain tiles were also used to clad the exterior of shops and pubs but again sometimes decorative panels or, for example, the name of the shop owner or licensee in tile form can be found.

The choice of where to use tiles in the building and what kind of tiles were to be used was usually left to the architect and the builder. In the case of prestigious buildings the architect would specify the architectural detail including ornamental features. Many tile firms would carry out special tile commissions designed by architects, and craft potters like William De Morgan, who made beautiful hand-painted tiles of great aesthetic worth, would be asked to supply a certain quantity for special clients. The builders of the vast majority of houses, however, had to rely on the mass-produced tile and yet still had a great deal of choice because tile firms would send around catalogues showing the range of tiles held in stock. The many tiles found in ordinary Victorian houses are therefore probably the choice of the builder rather than of the architect or the occupant, since on architectural drawings such details as tiles are not usually specified and so were left to the builder's discretion. So builders who favoured tiles

would use them more liberally than builders who had no special liking for them. On the backs of tiles one can sometimes come across directions written in pencil by the builder of where a specific batch of tiles was to be used.

Among the many new tile producers which sprang up during the 1870s, 1880s and 1890s are such names as Craven Dunnill and Company, the Campbell Brick and Tile Company, Sherwin and Cotton, and Pilkingtons Tile and Pottery Company Limited, but the firm which eventually outpaced them all was the already well established Maw and Company. They moved their Benthall works in Broseley to Jackfield near Ironbridge in 1883 and there the firm grew to become the biggest producer of tiles in Britain, exporting to Europe, Asia and America. They marketed a full range of inlaid tiles, plain and decorated wall tiles and a large range of architectural faience. Their resident designer, Charles Henry Temple, designed individual tiles as well as large panels. The firm took part in many international exhibitions and had a very large stand at the World's Fair in 1893 in Chicago. Their name was well known in many European countries despite competition from several important tile manufacturers in countries such as Belgium (Boch Frères), Germany (Villeroy and Boch) and France (De Smet

The tiled frontage of a butcher's shop in Leeds with the owner's name and the heads of a ram and a ewe, c 1890.

One of Carter and Company's tile decorators painting a panel, c 1895 (taken from W. J. Furnival's 'Leadless Decorative Tiles, Faience and Mosaic', 1904).

Women workers decorating tiles at Carter and Company, Poole, Dorset, c 1895 (taken from W. J. Furnival's 'Leadless Decorative Tiles, Faience and Mosaic' 1904)

et Cie). They, however, could not match the extensive range of ware produced by Maw and Company. Maw remained a formidable producer of tiles well into the twentieth century.

If Maw and Company, and to a certain extent Mintons China Works as well, managed to penetrate the European market against local competition, a few Dutch tilemakers managed to take a very small share of the British market during the period 1870-1900. No British tile manufacturer made hand-produced tin-glazed tiles in the fashion of the seventeenth and eighteenth centuries. Two Dutch firms in particular, J. van Hulst in Harlingen, Friesland, and Ravestyen in Utrecht, captured a small share of the British market by making the normally smaller Dutch Delftware tile the same size as the standard British tile, which is 6 inches (152mm), and thus enabling their product to be used in British cast iron fireplaces and furniture. Moreover, no tilemaker could match their hand-made product in its design and glazing technique, and so they were able to find an export market where no other foreign tilemaker could succeed. The Dutch tile designs found in Britain fall into two categories: conventional Dutch Delftware designs going back to the seventeenth and eighteenth centuries with the only difference of added colour in the form of green, purple, orange, yellow and blue, rather than the traditional all blue or all purple designs on a white ground; and designs that were very much inspired by the English Arts and Crafts movement. The influence of William Morris was keenly felt in Holland at the end of the nineteenth century and certain tile designs show this clearly. This was another reason for the relative popularity of this type of tile in Britain, since the Dutch tiles were made and decorated by hand in keeping with the philosophy of the Arts and Crafts

A selection of tiles made by Maw and Company: (top to bottom and left to right) inlaid tile, brown, buff, green, blue and white, c 1880; inlaid tile, buff and brown, c 1875; inlaid tile, blue, buff and white, c 1875; blue-green transfer print, c 1885; black transfer print, green and purple, c 1885; moulded portrait tile, c 1883.

15

movement. It is odd to think that England exported its Arts and Crafts ideas to the continent and that once absorbed by such a native industry as Dutch tilemaking they were exported again to Britain to find a place in the history of late Victorian tiles.

Although the Victorian era ended in 1901, the making of decorative tiles continued unabated into the Edwardian age. During this time Art Nouveau tiles became very popular, particularly relief tiles. Producing tiles with a relief design is very simple indeed. If, during the dust-pressing process, a plate with a design in reversed relief is used, the tile will come out of the press with a raised design on the surface — a good example of how tiles can be made and decorated in a single operation. It is also an example of the increased mechanisation in the tile industry, where labour-saving devices continued to be developed. Once the tile with the raised design was fired it could be coated with a single translucent glaze or several different glazes could be applied. This process had to be done by hand in most instances.

Few new tile firms were established during the Edwardian period. A notable exception was H. and R. Johnson Limited, who set up their Crystal Tile Works at Cobridge in Staffordshire in 1901. Through a series of takeovers and amalgamations they have now become the largest tile manufacturer in Britain. They were responsible for the creation of the ceramic tile gallery at the Gladstone Pottery Museum, Longton, Stoke-on-Trent, which is still the only tile gallery which shows the history of the ceramic tile from the middle ages to the present day, concentrating to a great extent on the Victorian period.

OPPOSITE: A selection of Craven Dunnill tiles: (top to bottom and left to right) brown block-printed tile, c 1890; green block-printed tile, c 1890; two border tiles measuring 6 by 3 inches (152 by 76 mm); green transfer-printed tile, c 1890; brown block-printed tile, c 1890; moulded tile with maiolica glazes, c 1880.

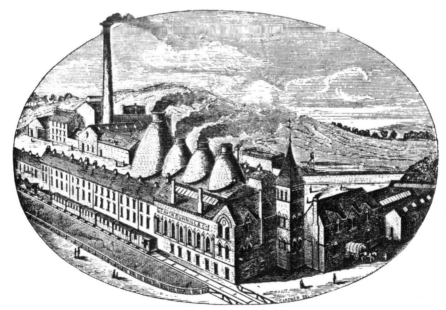

An engraving showing a view of Craven Dunnill's tile works at Jackfield near Ironbridge, c 1875 (taken from L. Jewitt's 'The Ceramic Art of Great Britain', 1878).

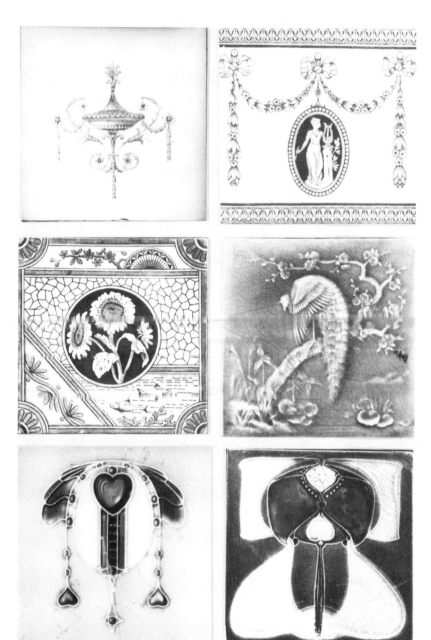

A range of tiles based on classical, oriental and Art Nouveau designs: (top to bottom and left to right) blue transfer, T. and R. Boote Limited, c 1885; blue transfer, Wedgwood, c 1890; brown transfer, T. A. Simpson and Company, 1881; moulded oriental design, Minton,blue, c 1880; moulded Art Nouveau design, pale green, blue and brown, H. and R. Johnson, 1908; moulded Art Nouveau design, pale green, dark green and red, c 1905.

Neo-Gothic tiles for church use showing the influence of medieval design: (top to bottom and left to right) inlaid tile with fleur-de-lis, Minton, c 1870; inlaid tile with winged ox (Saint Luke), Campbell Brick and Tile Company, c 1885; tiles with letters inlaid based on Gothic script, Campbell Brick and Tile Company, c 1885.

STYLES AND THEMES

Victorian attitudes to design are strongly reflected in the many different styles discernible in Victorian tiles. Perhaps the word 'style' within a Victorian context is a misnomer since the Victorians did not really have a style of their own but borrowed indiscriminately from the past. There were many so called grammars of ornament which provided designers and architects with a plethora of examples ranging from Egyptian times up to the Baroque period, neatly arranged in chronological order. It was then a matter of straight copying or adapting designs which suited your particular need. Among this multitude of sources, two historical styles were particularly popular, the Graeco-Roman and Gothic. In the case of better class architec-

Two hand-made and hand-painted panels by the Arts and Crafts potter William De Morgan, made sometime between 1888 and 1897. The sensitive quality of design is clearly evident.

ture, which was usually designed in one style or another, it followed that any tiles used reflected the style of the building. Gothic Revival churches feature floor tiles with inlaid designs based on geometrical Gothic motifs, quatrefoils and fleurs-de-lis, while buildings based on Greek or Roman styles would have tiles with classical symmetrical arrangements often incorporating stylised flowers and animals or in the form of more pictorial panels representing such things as the muses, Greek and Roman gods or personifications of the four winds and the elements. Tiles in buildings based on Egyptian, Byzantine,

Romanesque or Renaissance examples would follow similar patterns.

It was not only the historical past which attracted the attention of the Victorian designer, but the designs of the Middle East and Far East became sources of inspiration too. Japanese and Persian designs in particular added an exotic touch to the already extensive historical repertoire of forms and shapes. One of the few highlights in the history of Victorian tile design came in the person of William De Morgan. De Morgan was closely associated with William Morris, founder of the Arts and Crafts movement. They aimed at designs of high

An interesting underwater scene with fish and water beetles, brown transfer, pale yellow and green, Minton Hollins and Company, c 1880.

Tiles with birds, animals and landscapes are popular among collectors: (top to bottom and left to right) bird, brown transfer, blue, yellow and green, c 1885; turkey, inlaid, buff and brown, Campbell Brick and Tile Company, c 1885; hare, blue, Wedgwood, c 1880; deer, moulded, brown, c 1890; landscape with windmill, black transfer, green and brown, c 1880; landscape with Bay of Naples, brown transfer, c 1870.

Scenes with children, portraits and scenes from literature are always very attractive: (top to bottom and left to right) boys playing marbles, brown transfer, Malkin Edge, c 1895; little boy and head of cat, black transfer, Minton Hollins and Company, c 1880; medieval lady, dark brown transfer, E. Smith and Company, c 1885; Victorian girl, colour transfer, c 1890; scene from 'Macbeth', black transfer, Mintons China Works, designed by M. Smith, c 1880; Sleeping Beauty, brown transfer, Mintons China Works, designed by M. Smith, c 1880.

Two floral tiles: (left) sgraffito tile (design scratched through a thin layer of clay), Flaxman, c 1890; (right) Art Nouveau tile, hand-painted, dark brown, red and green, c 1900.

quality, which although drawn from a variety of sources (medieval, Persian and so on) showed a very personal stamp and developed sensitivity for design. In keeping with the Arts and Crafts philosophy De Morgan's tiles were both made and decorated by hand and their excellent design and beautiful colour put them in a class of their own.

Another interesting late stylistic development was Art Nouveau. Art Nouveau tiles have sinuous designs (whiplash style) based on plant forms, flowers, and sometimes birds like peacocks. They are invariably executed as relief designs decorated with bright translucent glazes which create a strong visual impact. There are also tiles with straightforward naturalistic representations of flowers or animals which do not fall into the category of historical or exotic styles.

In the Victorian era the variety of subject matter is far greater than that of any earlier or later period in the history of tiles. Flowers, birds, animals, landscapes, scenes from literature, portraits and scenes from daily life were all represented on tiles. Pictorial tiles of this nature are now keenly collected by museums and private individuals and they provide a fascinating field of study. The most common subject matter derives from flowers. Treatment can either be an exact depiction of a particular flower or can be in the form of a semi-abstract pattern based on flowers. Flowers have been a source of inspiration for

24

A selection of transfer-printed and hand-coloured tiles depicting a variety of different flowers. The dates of the tiles range from 1885 to 1895.

25

designers in most historical periods, and so they appear even more frequently in Victorian design since designers then borrowed so freely from the past. The variety is so great that it is quite feasible to build up a collection of Victorian flower tiles which would show the whole range of decoration techniques, stylistic periods and different species.

Birds are an intriguing theme, particularly within a stylistic context. Tiles influenced by the Far East often show birds among branches with blossom; tiles based on medieval designs often have simplified bird forms reminiscent of doves or eagles, which are connected with Christian symbolism or medieval heraldry; there are tiles with very accurate naturalistic depictions of birds often in colour, and there are the dazzling and splendidly colourful peacocks from the Art Nouveau period.

Animals are an equally fascinating theme. There are tiles which depict deer, dogs, lions, hares, rabbits or monkeys and tiles that show animals within a literary context (for example Aesop's fables). William De Morgan, the Arts and Crafts potter, produced many tiles showing an interesting variety of animals and these are now much sought after.

Landscape tiles have popular appeal whether they be scenes from faraway places or pictures of local beauty spots. The same applies to scenes from literature. Shakespeare and the well known fairy stories were frequent sources for designers such as Moyr Smith, who worked for Mintons China Works. He created a catalogue of pictorial tiles in which the human figure forms the chief motif. These now occupy an important place in the history of Victorian pictorial tiles.

Scenes from daily life range from farmyard scenes, trades and occupations to hunting scenes and children at play, but like portrait tiles, which show well known Victorians or famous men and women of the past, they are not very numerous and therefore usually expensive.

COLLECTING TILES

Collecting Victorian tiles has now become an established pursuit. Most people start by accident — by finding a few tiles left in the house by a previous occupant, or by having some tiles *in situ* in the house, or by falling in love with a tile in an antique shop. It can become an enjoyable and at times exciting pastime. It is important from the outset to determine what kind of collection you want to build up. The field is large, and knowing what you want will save you time and money. Anybody interested in the whole history of Victorian tiles can still form a reasonable collection showing a facet of every important aspect of that history. The first requirement is to know something of the general history of Victorian tiles and there are several books (see page 32) which go into reasonable detail while covering the overall picture. In the end you will be collecting a few examples of every known decorative technique, subject matter, style and manufacturer. This would be enough to keep you busy for a lifetime, but if you restrict yourself to, say, two examples of each category, it is feasible. You might even want to include a few examples of earlier periods to show the historical lead-up to the Victorian tile.

The other possibility is to specialise in one category. You might like floral tiles and concentrate on them exclusively, although you would have scope within that category to see that your specimens illustrate decoration techniques and styles. An Art Nouveau tile with a lily is very different in stylistic treatment and technical execution from an inlaid tile with a fleur-de-lis based on medieval examples

OPPOSITE: *A selection of Victorian tiles showing different styles, subject matter and decoration techniques: (top to bottom and left to right) floral tile, yellow incised lines in red body, Maw and Company, c 1885; floral tile, hand-painted with slip, c 1880; Neo-Gothic inlaid tile, Campbell Brick and Tile Company, c 1880; head of cherub moulded in relief, green glaze, Sherwin and Cotton, c 1895; scene depicting Loch Long, colour transfer, c 1890; Art Nouveau tile, green glaze, c 1905.*

PATTERNS OF ART PAINTED AND ENAMELLED TILES FOR FURNITURE, FRIEZES, AND OTHER MURAL DECORATION.

MANUFACTORY & SHOWROOMS,
MINTON, HOLLINS & Co.,
Patent Tile Works,
STOKE-UPON-TRENT.

SCALE—1¼ INCHES TO A FOOT.

LONDON HOUSE & SHOWROOMS,
MINTON & Co.,
50, Conduit St., Regent St., W.

ABOVE: *Some tiles have useful information on the back and this tile has as much as one could wish for: the name of the maker ('Mintons China Works'), the place of manufacture ('Stoke on Trent'), the country of origin ('Made in England'), the Minton trade mark, catalogue pattern number ('No 2684') and a registration number ('Rd No 219706'), which gives us an approximate date of 1894.*
OPPOSITE: *A page from a Minton catalogue of the 1880s. The many gold medals are proof of Minton's production of good-quality tiles over many years.*

and yet they both belong to your chosen theme of flowers. If that is still too wide a field for your liking, you may want to concentrate on naturalistically printed and painted flowers only, of which there is an abundance of examples. The good thing about a theme like flowers is that the tiles within this category are fairly common and therefore not expensive. Collecting tiles with children's fairy tales or nursery rhymes would be an expensive hobby, although here it would be a matter of

quality rather than quantity. Collecting Victorian tiles can suit all pockets, and every line of approach brings its own rewards.

The commonest source for tiles is the antique shop. It is a challenge to build up a good collection without paying inflated prices, and often you come across similar tiles in different shops at very different prices, so a shrewd collector does not rush into the first antique shop arrived at. The more experienced collector often finds an antique shop where the prices are reasonable or the owner is willing to bargain with him. In the end everybody benefits by it, since you get tiles at reasonable prices and the dealer knows you will come back. Once antique shop owners get to know you as a regular customer they might even look out for special tiles and keep them aside for you or give you tips where something of interest is available. You may also come across tiles in flea markets, and at times they may be available from demolition sites, but this can only be done after consulting the demolition contractor. It is certainly worth trying since you know exactly what the tile has been used for and the date of the house is often a fair guide to the date of the tile.

The basic questions most collectors will ask themselves are: how old are my tiles, who made them, and how were they made? These can often be answered by looking carefully at the tile itself. The back of the tile can often provide a lot of information about its date and manufacturer. Some manufacturers printed or impressed their names on the back together with the place of manufacture, for example *Maw & Co, Benthall Works, Broseley, Salop.* The same information can also be incorporated in a trade mark but again the essential details are there. The type of name or trade mark usually varied over a period of time. Maw and Company, for example, used various trade marks between 1850 and 1900 which also give an indication of the date. Other clues to the date can be found on the back in the form of printed registration marks. Between 1842 and 1883 diamond-shaped marks with letters and numbers were used: the various letters stand for certain years and months and with the right key (which can be found in most guides to pottery and tiles) it is simple to find the year and month of registration, giving you an approximate date of the tile. After 1883 a consecutive series of numbers was used and again it is possible from a range of numbers to find a particular year. It is also important to remember that most Victorian wall tiles were made after 1880, while the inlaid tiles can date back to 1840 or so.

Determining how your tiles were made and decorated is at times complex but most tiles fall into certain main categories. One basic distinction lies between floor tiles, usually inlaid, and wall tiles, though inlaid tiles are at times also used on the wall. Inlaid tiles are usually thicker and heavier than wall tiles. They look and are very strong objects intended to withstand a lot of hard wear. A good inlaid floor tile does last a long time, as can still be seen in town halls and other public buildings. Many inlaid tiles look like a sandwich when seen from the side. This arises from an economy dodge on the part of the maker, who used fine clay on the outside where it showed and coarser clay in the middle. This sandwich process tended to improve the strength of the tile and helped to avoid warping.

Wall tiles are usually 6 inches (152 mm) square, although 8 inch (203 mm) varieties are not uncommon. Border tiles can measure 3 by 6 inches (76 by 152 mm) or even 1 by 6 inches (25 by 153 mm). Wall tiles are usually $\frac{3}{8}$ inch (10 mm) thick but this can vary from manufacturer to manufacturer. Wall tiles are much more numerous than inlaid tiles and a further difference is that wall tiles are usually made from dust-pressed clay. Tiles made by that process are very smooth and regular while tiles made from plastic clay tend to be a little uneven at times. Most tilemakers dust-pressed their tiles but certain firms like Copeland and Burmantofts and craft potters like De Morgan cut their tiles from plastic clay. Transfer printing is a common decoration technique and the print is usually under a thin layer of transparent glaze. Transfer-printed tiles come in two varieties, plain transfer-printed tiles, and transfer-printed with added hand colour. In the plain variety one usually finds a printed image in black, brown and sometimes red and green. It was possible to add ceramic colour to the printed image by hand. Tiles with broad flat printed images were usually done by a method called blockprinting. In this case the image is transferred from a metal plate on which the design stands out in relief. More than one colour can be used but then more plates are needed. The process of making inlaid tiles and dust-pressed tiles with the design stamped in relief on the surface has already been described and most tiles are decorated in this way or by the transfer-printing process, but there were also still some hand

Tiles can be displayed effectively against a background of dark cork and held secure with a few steel nails. They can also stand or lie on a shelf.

processes used. One of these is slip painting, by which a tile is painted with various coloured slips (thin liquid clay) and after firing coated with a translucent glaze and fired again. It is also possible to trail thin lines of slip on a tile and after the first firing fill the areas between the raised slip lines with translucent glazes. These tiles took longer to produce and were usually more expensive.

Gaining knowledge of decoration techniques can only be done at first hand by looking hard at tiles at close quarters. A collector can build up his experience in four ways: by reading specialised literature on the subject; by studying tile collections in museums; by looking at tiles *in situ*; and, probably most usefully, by studying his own collection and pursuing any unanswered questions until the problem has been solved. It is very rewarding to find the answer to a particular enigma after long hours of detective work. The field of studying Victorian tiles is relatively new. Owing to the highly complex and specialised nature of modern scholarship, few fields for original research remain open to the amateur. The subject of Victorian tiles is one such.

PLACES TO VISIT
Museums with tiles on permanent display are listed below:

Birmingham City Museum and Art Gallery, Congreve Street, Birmingham. Telephone: 021-235 2834. Islamic tiles, eighteenth-century tiles, and tiles made by William De Morgan.

British Museum, Great Russell Street, London WC1. Telephone: 01 636 1555 Large collection of medieval tiles.

City Museum and Art Gallery, Broad Street, Hanley, Stoke-on-Trent. Telephone: Stoke-on-Trent (0782) 29611. Major collections of ceramics including tiles.

Gladstone Pottery Museum, Uttoxeter Road, Longton, Stoke-on-Trent. Telephone: Stoke-on-Trent (0782) 310322. Tile gallery showing the development of tiles from the middle ages to the present day.

Ironbridge Gorge Museum, Ironbridge, Telford. Telephone: Ironbridge (095 245) 3522. Tiles made by Maw and Company and Craven Dunnill can be seen at Maw's Benthall Works, Jackfield, near Ironbridge.

Manchester City Art Gallery, Mosley Street, Manchester. Telephone: 061-236 9422. A fine collection of eighteenth-century wall tiles with printed decorations by John Sadler and Guy Green of Liverpool.

Minton Museum, Royal Doulton Tableware Limited, London Road, Stoke-on-Trent. Collection of Minton tiles.

People's Palace Museum, Glasgow Green, Glasgow. Telephone: 041-554 0223. Victorian tiles and picture panels.

Victoria and Albert Museum, Cromwell Road, South Kensington, London SW7. Telephone: 01-589 6371. Large collection of Persian, Turkish, British medieval, Italian, Dutch, Spanish and English Delftware tiles. They also have a fine collection of tiles made by William De Morgan.

FURTHER READING

Austwick, J. and B. *The Decorated Tile*. Pitman House, 1980.
Barnard, J. *Victorian Ceramic Tiles*. Studio Vista, 1972.
Berendsen, A. *Tiles — A General History*. Faber and Faber, 1967.
Lemmen, H. van. *Tiles — A Collector's Guide*. Souvenir Press, 1979.
Lockett, T. A. *Collecting Victorian Tiles*. Antique Collectors' Club, 1979.